If you don't get feedback
from your performers
and your audience,
you're going to be
working in a vacuum.

~Peter Maxwell Davies

HEY LEADER,
WAKE UP AND HEAR THE FEEDBACK!

ERIC HARVEY
AND
145 OF YOUR COLLEAGUES, MANAGERS, AND DIRECT REPORTS

WALKTHETALK.COM
Resources for Personal and Professional Success

To order additional copies of this handbook, or for information
about other WALK THE TALK® products and services,
contact us at
1.888.822.9255
or visit
www.walkthetalk.com

HEY LEADER, WAKE UP AND HEAR THE FEEDBACK

The WALK THE TALK Company
1100 Parker Square, Suite 250
Flower Mound, TX. 75028
972.899.8300

WALK THE TALK books may be purchased for educational, business, or sales promotion use.

Printed in the United States of America
10 9 8 7 6 5 4 3 2 1

Printed by MultiAd

$14.95
ISBN 978-1-885228-88-8
51495>

9 781885 228888

CONTENTS

INTRODUCTION

Another typical book about leadership?

Not hardly!

To be sure, there are literally thousands of books on the subject of leadership. Most have been written by one or two authors with various business and/or academic backgrounds who share their views of what it takes to lead other people through a myriad of strategies, models, and formulas. The reality, however, is that many of those resources are not as helpful or easy to follow as intended. The good news: This book is different! Its approach is rather unique and so are the sources of the information provided.

In order to create **Hey Leader** and ensure it was as "real world" and practical as possible, we turned to those who truly know and understand what effective leadership feels and looks like. We surveyed thousands of working individuals from a full range of professions, experiences, and geographic locations – asking them one simple question:

> ***Based on your experience, what is it that truly effective and highly respected leaders DO?***

Over 500 responses were received from employees, team members, and leaders from all levels around the world – of which 145 were selected and assembled within the 10 topic chapters that comprise this work.

Hey Leader, Wake Up and Hear the Feedback! will provide you and your colleagues with powerful and important information which – if you're willing to really hear it – can enhance your growth, personal development, and professional success. Using it for that purpose is the very best way to thank the people who have willingly shared their thoughts and ideas with you.

To get the greatest benefit from this valuable collection, consider reading with a marker in hand. Highlight key lines that resonate with you … ideas to remember … thoughts that match your own experiences and perceptions of leadership throughout your life. Then periodically go back and review those highlights as real-world reminders of what you need to be doing in order to be the best leader possible.

Many years ago, my colleague and friend Ken Blanchard coined the phrase (and mantra) "Feedback is the breakfast of champions." Those words ring as true today as they did when Ken first uttered them. So get ready to enjoy, and benefit from, a 145-course feast!

Eric Harvey, President
The WALK THE TALK® Company
walkthetalk.com

Learning and Development

The growth and development of people
is the highest calling of leadership.

~ Harvey S. Firestone

An effective leader should always prepare the next person to take on a leadership role. A good way to do this is to identify a potential leader on your team. When the leader has been identified, talk with the person to ensure they have the same goals that you have for them. If both of you agree, start working with that person by setting expectations, encouraging leadership courses, attending meetings with you – or in your place, assigning high-level duties, and be open if he or she has a different way of approaching situations than you.

Kathy Ibrahim, Burlington, North Carolina

Many leaders are so busy leading that they neglect to take time to think, vision, plan, and develop themselves as people.

Tommy Echols, Cicero, New York

Remember that knowledge and experience are not for your secret memory file. When you have the benefit of knowledge and experience, don't brag about them or use them as weapons for chastising your team. Instead, use them as tools for development. Share your knowledge and experience so that others may learn. It does not take anything away from you, and can come back to you in multiple ways through the success of your team.

Nancy Springler, New Orleans, Louisiana

Identify and develop successors. Leaders should not only be concerned with the success of their team, organization, and company while they are there – they should also be focused on making sure those groups are set up for success after they are gone. The best way to do that is to have a solid succession plan. Identify one or two people who display the potential to possibly succeed you. Meet with them to make sure they are interested in a future leadership role. Discuss ideas for development, provide appropriate resources (training, books, mentoring), and find them some stretch opportunities. You cannot wait until you are ready to leave to consider who will replace you. Sometimes that is out of your control. The best leaders are always looking for and working with those who will come behind them so they are positioned for years of future success.

Willie Ryder, Charlotte, North Carolina

One behavior all effective leaders share is a strong sense of self-awareness. This form of awareness provides not only insight about their strengths and limitations, but also of how their actions are perceived by the people they serve. It's difficult to offer recognition or understand what matters to those you lead if you lack an awareness of what you're communicating through your words and actions. Likewise, it becomes more challenging to empathize with how challenges are affecting your team if you're not aware of how they're also impacting your leadership. Having this self-awareness of your leadership, and what's expected from you in this role, is critical to understanding how you can help lead others toward achieving a common goal.

Tanveer Naseer, Montreal, Quebec

As an author, speaker, and writers' group leader, I've learned that while it's great to be organized, goal oriented, and enthusiastic, be wary of enjoying the sound of your own voice. A violin solo may be beautiful but lacks the strength of many instruments blended into a mighty orchestra. Become a group maestro by making eye contact and being aware of body language and the emotion behind the words. An active listener absorbs and repeats or rephrases the speaker's words and seeks clarification: "So what I'm hearing you say is ... Is that right?" Remember: Effective Leaders Listen!

Virginia Nygard, Port St. Lucie, Florida

Because we are unable to meet with our individual agents and employees daily, we spend 8–12 hours each week in preparation for one meeting involving all of them. The intense preparation affords us the opportunity to conduct a professionally styled presentation that creates value for each individual. Each presentation is informational, motivational, and instructional. This is difficult to do in a challenging business climate, but it can be done if we are willing to dedicate the time. We have come to the conclusion that if we are going to get the attention of our people for 45 minutes a week for a meeting, then we are going to make the very most of it.

Dana Potter, Westlake Village, California

Truly effective leaders must be **PRESENT!** With the pace of change, globalization, technology advancements, and doing more with less, whatever happened to management by walking around? Too often in today's environment, leaders are so distracted that they are disconnected as to what is happening with their people. One-on-ones are put off for other "strategic priorities" and performance feedback is infrequent – missing opportunities for meaningful, timely, and productive personal development discussions. All of this can lead to a distrusting, disjointed, and disenchanted environment.

Effective leaders are accessible and present; they consistently engage with their people, give their people their full attention, view their people as a priority, and develop them accordingly. They align their actions with their words, do what they say they are going to do, and equally reward good performance, as well as uphold the consequences for poor performance.

Effective communication – an essential attribute of leadership – can often be lost in today's fast-paced world of technology! Don't miss the opportunities that managing by walking around can reveal! When was the last time you stopped by the desk of a direct report and asked, "How are things going? ... What can I do to help?" Your **PRESENCE** matters!

Tasha Delaney, East Fallowfield, Pennsylvania

My goal is to make my team members more effective – and prepare them to become my bosses through the use of the **5 "E"s**. **E**mpathize, **E**ncourage, **E**ducate, **E**mpower, and **E**xpect.

Freddie Cogburn, Maryville, Tennessee

Give a detailed and accurate annual review with feedback from the entire year. Annual reviews are vital to an employee's growth and success. Reviews should highlight the good and include goals to help employees improve and/or take things to the next level. Keep a file for each employee and fill it with successes, challenges, accomplishments, etc. throughout the year. Then reference this file when completing the review to make sure nothing is left out. Keep in mind that nothing should be a surprise to an employee during a review.

Stacey Lubash, Omaha, Nebraska

Support others in reaching their own goals by asking them on a regular basis how they are getting on with the task at hand and offer them your help or experience if they need it. You could perhaps give them an example of a project you were working on and how someone else helped you meet your goal.

Julia Reedshaw, Leeds, West Yorkshire, UK

As a manager,
Act with the understanding that your
management role has an objective
of developing and encouraging others to
succeed by doing the right task at the right
time … every day … every week … every
month … to become the best they
can possibly be.

212° – the extra degree
a walkthetalk.com publication

Truly effective leaders expect the best from their employees. Learn your employees' strengths and build on them by giving challenging opportunities to grow those strengths. Tell employees how much as a leader you believe in them and what they can accomplish. Give them specific tasks or opportunities, provide them with the time and tools to be successful; praise them for the accomplishment when they achieve their best. You will grow more positive team members and have more resources for future projects.

It's important to match organizational needs with what the employee can achieve; start with simpler, short-term opportunities and build on them. If employees know you believe in them to accomplish great things, they will begin to believe in themselves.

Dayna Harbin, Springfield, Missouri

The most important task of an effective leader is to **LEAD YOURSELF**. Leading yourself involves being intentional about developing your "Head" (intellect), your "Heart" (character), and your "Hands" (skills). To cultivate your intellect – "leaders are readers." To cultivate your heart – leaders focus on their emotional intelligence – the most important factor of effective leadership. To cultivate your skills – leaders are practitioners. Leadership expert Dee Hock states, "It is management of self that should occupy 50% of our time and the best of our ability." If you cannot lead yourself, how can you lead others?

Dr. Craig Domeck, Orlando, Florida

A good, effective leader is generous in **SHARING** his or her knowledge, skills, and experience and must not be threatened by young, good, and upcoming subordinates. Instead, the leader should see them as potential recipients of "the baton" as he/she prepares for bigger and better opportunities within the organization or elsewhere.

Estelita S. Ocampo, Makati City, Philippines

SUCCESSion Planning: Truly effective leaders recognize that the cornerstone of their success – and of the success of those they work for and with – is to continuously identify and develop internal employees who show the potential to fill key leadership positions in the company, now and in the future. They seek expertise on the one hand and recognize leadership qualities on the other. They actively create opportunities for potential successors to contribute, learn, and grow with the focused purpose of developing the leaders of tomorrow – leaders who will be ready to assume greater responsibilities and accountabilities with confidence, savvy, and aplomb. This is as true of emergent leaders as of seasoned ones.

Angela Hinton, Toronto, Ontario

Effective leaders "mentor" effortlessly, and very naturally, the employees whom they consider their most valuable assets. It can be argued that every employee – regardless of age or experience – needs mentoring. Typically, we think of an older, more experienced person leading a new, less experienced "protégé" through the hurdles of a new experience. However, mentoring need not be confined to these limited parameters. A good leader sees mentoring as a part of every relationship he or she has with every employee. By embracing the mentoring role, a good leader can feel comfortable soliciting feedback, giving positive reinforcement, and consciously (or unconsciously) creating a positive flow of energy that results in the employee feeling vital to the smooth workings of the organization.

Jane Van Horne, Campbellton, New Brunswick

One thing that truly effective leaders do is "never forget the last step they took up the ladder of success." This is a simple concept but one that too often is forgotten as managers move up within an organization. The easiest way to practice this idea is to let those whom you manage know that you are concerned with and support hearing about any obstacles they face day in and day out. You can't simply say, "I understand" or "I know what you are going through"; you have to listen to the issues and then act on them by either providing solutions from your own experiences or reaching out to others to provide solutions or suggestions. This is key in building a trusting and engaged team.

Jason Mueller, Norman, Oklahoma

Energizing and Engaging Others

If your actions inspire others to dream more,
learn more, do more, and become more,
you are a leader.

~ John Quincy Adams

Ask Three Questions for Successful Change. All leaders introduce ideas they hope will gain acceptance. Effective leaders don't wait to guess what people are thinking. They go out to those affected, explain the idea in person, share the thinking behind it, and then ask this magical question: *What's important to you about* _____? This draws out areas of agreement, disagreement, and misunderstanding. Most of all, the discussion that follows builds ownership through engagement. The next leadership question. *What would you do differently about* _____? refines the idea and further increases ownership through participation. Finally, a closing question: *How would you proceed with this to make it work*? When energy builds around the responses, the new idea is well on its way. Why? Because this simple question is all about implementation. When people start discussing the "how," the idea has turned into action.

Steve Roesler, Medford, New Jersey

The most important thing any leader can do to create a motivating environment is to make sure the work every member of the team is doing is meaningful. When you believe what you are doing is making a difference, it's energizing. On the other hand, there's no worse feeling than knowing your work just doesn't matter. Every leader has some degree of discretion in being able to eliminate or minimize the amount of "muda" (non-value-added work) that flows into a team. Any job can be strategic. Maybe you've heard the story of the two bricklayers – one of them saw his job as stacking bricks; the other saw his mission as building a magnificent cathedral. Same job – different worldview! Making sure work is meaningful is the best form of job security a leader can give a team. If the work is important, it's less likely to be eliminated.

Dan McCarthy, Durham, New Hampshire

Over the 20+ years I've been in business, I've had opportunities to look behind the scenes of literally thousands of organizations of various sizes and industries. I've noticed one factor common to those companies that realize rapid growth: their leaders have a clear vision for the future and share that vision openly with their teams. This one thing seems to result in faster decision-making at all levels and a greater commitment by team members. It also makes recruiting the right people much easier and encourages people to be more focused on teamwork vs. individual performance. By contrast, companies whose leaders do not have a clear vision or fail to share their vision with team members often stagnate or see minimal growth.

Sharon Hayes, Cornwall, Ontario

Truly Effective Leaders engage to the **"H.I.L.T."**

They show their Humanity and sense of "oneness" with those they lead through their actions and words.

They demonstrate genuine Interest in the ideas and individuals from whom those ideas come from by establishing a dynamic working connectivity in an open and inclusive environment.

They Listen for understanding, meaning, clarity, and content and always demonstrate a sincere appreciation to those willing to share ideas, thoughts, and feelings.

They establish Trust as the primary basis of the relationship, which enables effective leadership and optimal followership.

Being an Effective Leader means being ready to engage to the **H.I.L.T**!

Kenneth Morton, Charlotte, North Carolina

Effective leaders are masterfully able to communicate. This communication – whether verbal or electronic – is reinforced through consistency, which helps create a sense of stability as well as security. Furthermore, effective leaders create an environment in which all employees feel like they report to a superior – but this same superior truly works to increase efficiency and effectiveness of daily business operations. In this regard, an effective leader may be a subordinate. These are individuals not defined by titles but by actions; individuals who do not merely understand, believe, achieve, or deliver – they consistently "over-stand," over-believe, over-achieve, and over-deliver.

Tonjua "TJ" Jones, Oro Valley, Arizona

Recognize an employee's good work in staff meetings when you hear from an internal or external customer that your employee gave service over and above what was expected. At a call center where I work as a quality assurance coordinator, we had a "High Five Club" bulletin board on which an employee's picture and compliments were posted.

Velma O. Willard, Boerne, Texas

Listen to the intelligence that lies within the room. Openly encourage your staff to willingly challenge your way of thinking which in turn will encourage growth on a personal and business level.

Bill Elmer, The Hills District, NSW, Australia

Truly effective leaders empower their employees to make decisions. When leaders make all of the small decisions, they have effectively paralyzed themselves by forcing their teams into dependent states. Their teams can very easily become dependent to the point of lacking the confidence to make even the smallest calls. When this happens, a leader's office becomes a revolving door of constant interruption. He or she has no time to look at the big picture and drive the direction of the team – becoming too caught up in details instead of the direction. Allowing and even requiring a team to make decisions will free up a leader's time so that he or she can focus on the "forest" instead of the "trees." Delegating these decisions will also instill a sense of ownership and responsibility in team members and lead to better results and greater accountability on an ongoing basis.

Jodie Beyer, Odessa, Texas

Empower Your Team Members – by asking for their input and then removing barriers. Soliciting team member ideas in areas where they have expertise motivates and empowers them. Every member has valuable input and contributions to offer. The keys are to ask, listen, and understand what they are suggesting, and then remove barriers that could stand in the way of their accomplishment. When team members are asked for input and know it will be used (or at least considered), they are careful to give the best suggestions – and to take an active ownership in both the work and the results. When a team knows their leader will step out ahead to remove barriers, they provide invaluable support to see the job through with quality results.

Sandy Stewart, San Jose, California

RESEARCH STATISTICS

Here are just a few highlights from the volume of studies done globally which show a positive relationship or correlation between employee engagement and business performance ...

- Highly engaged employees outperform their disengaged colleagues by 20–28%. *(The Conference Board)*

- Engaged employees generate 40%+ more revenue than disengaged ones. *(Hay Group)*

- 84% of highly engaged employees believe they can impact the quality of their company's work product compared with 31% of the disengaged. *(Towers Perrin)*

- 70% of engaged employees indicate they have a good understanding of how to meet customer needs, while only 17% of non-engaged employees say the same. *(Right Management)*

- 68% of the highly engaged believe they can impact costs in their job or unit vs. 19% of the disengaged. *(Towers Perrin)*

- Engaged employees take an average of nearly 60% fewer sick days per year than disengaged employees. *(Gallup)*

- Engaged employees are 87% less likely to leave the organization than the disengaged. *(Corporate Leadership Council)*

180 Ways to Build Employee Engagement
a walkthetalk.com publication

Effective leaders get employees AT ALL LEVELS involved in specific decisions. For example, how many times do you hear "I'm just the receptionist" or "I'm just A/P and not involved in making that decision." These people are part of the team and many times have some of the best, most practical ideas on how to improve a process or make someone's job easier. Simply mark your calendar, and make it a priority, to ask for opinions or ideas of employees in departments of all levels once or twice a week. It WILL strengthen morale and improve their confidence, as well as Team Performance. Then watch someone with a negative attitude become more positive – something for all of us to smile about, everyday!

Karen Malone, Gilbert, Arizona

Focus on doing the Right Stuff! All too often, marginal leaders expend an inordinate amount of attention on doing THINGS RIGHT and not enough time encouraging people to do the RIGHT THINGS. Excellent leaders understand, pay attention to, and celebrate results that are high-payoff outcomes – like providing high-quality customer service.

Steve Ventura, Dallas, Texas

EMPOWER your staff! There is no greater way of honoring your staff than to give them the gift of empowerment. I trust my team members and have told them, "Just make the decision; we will talk it through later if it's the wrong one." What I've learned is that if I've done my job and given them the training they need, they will do everything in their power to make the right call ... and 99.9% of the time, they do!

Nancy Klemmer, Lakeport, Michigan

Keep your employees motivated and create truly positive working relationships by changing your focus. Most leaders tend to focus on the negative and wait to catch people doing things wrong. This can have dire consequences and lead to low morale and energy levels in employees. And it can impact your "leadership brand" – creating the perception of being a bully who fails to tell anyone when they do something right. Instead, change your focus to a more positive one. Look out for the positives in employee behavior and when you observe them doing something well, let them know. Tell them what you have observed, how proud you are of them, and the positive effect their behavior is having on customers and the team. And be sure to encourage them to keep up the good work. Do this and you will be amazed at how much more positive behavior you will get in return.

Craig Timmins, Livingston, Scotland

A leader inspires people by demonstrating enthusiasm. Having enthusiasm means you greet your people with a smile; you make an effort to remember their names. When results are not what you want them to be, it is your job to remind everyone that what seems a failure is simply the reverse side of a solution. Sharing a personal experience lets them know you understand. Let them know: "I don't expect you not to make a mistakes; I expect you not to repeat them."

Helene Bulger, Winnipeg, Manitoba

Make employee recognition a daily priority. This is a skill you have to practice and continue to develop in order to be most effective and get the best results from your direct reports. Don't make the common mistake of assuming that employee recognition will come naturally for you. To make this a priority, I keep a spreadsheet listing all associates and what is important to them in regard to their individual career paths – and what their specific individual needs are for recognition. It also tracks the type of recognition that I have given to each and how often. It can be something as simple as sending a "great job" email, announcing their achievement in a team meeting, or deliver a handwritten thank you. Updating this information becomes routine and ensures that it remains a priority for me – ultimately leading to increased retention, loyalty, and productivity.

Keith Newport, Alpharetta, Georgia

Truly effective leaders come to grips with the notion that not everything matters. It is tempting to believe that every challenge, complaint, and issue that employees bring up needs action. The fact is, they don't. Wanting to solve all things wastes time and saps the energy of not only leaders, but also those around them who are forced to react each time they reach out to get answers for the employees who are sending them off on yet another rabbit trail. Often those issues resolve themselves, and the best way they come to resolution is if the employees, themselves, rectify them. To engender that level of empowerment, effective leaders respond with questions, not answers. Ask questions that cause employees to come to their own conclusions and then congratulate them on their great ideas. Then you can get on with the things that matter the very most.

Dennis Schroeder, Pensacola, Florida

The one thing truly effective leaders do is give control! Managers take control – leaders give it. Here are a few guiding principles that should prove helpful:

1. Believe in your people.
2. Let your people know you believe in them.
3. Inspect what you expect.
4. Practice situational leadership (change your style with each person and each task).
5. Take an active role and invest in your people's development.
6. Let your people know their growth and development are important to you.
7. Demonstrate the importance of their development by giving them opportunities for growth.
8. Develop the competence and confidence of your people so they are motivated to act on their own.
9. Take responsibility for making your people "winners."
10. Do not be a crutch for people but be a CATALYST for their growth and development.
11. Don't set people up for failure by telling them what to do and leave them on their own.

Paige Austin, New Braunfels, Texas

Attitudes
Carry the Day

It's your *attitude*, not just your *aptitude*,
that determines your ultimate *altitude*.

~ *Zig Ziglar*

It's been my experience that people achieve **100%** of what you expect of them. **IF YOU BELIEVE THEY'LL SUCCEED, THEY WILL!** Likewise, if you believe they'll fail, your very thoughts can create situations where this will be the case. Your beliefs about others have immense power. Doubt, apathy, and disbelief are toxic energies when applied to people and teams. As a leader, you have the choice to do it differently. Focus your attention on fostering elements that build people from the inside up. Find ways to help them see their potential. Show, by your words and actions, that you KNOW it can be done and they're the ones to do it (not someone else). Believe in your heart that they'll succeed, then build their resources so they can take action.

Natasha Fowler, South Canterbury, Aotearoa, New Zealand

If you want to be a truly effective leader, you must develop relationships that express genuine appreciation! How does that look you ask? Try this one thing: sit down and compose a handwritten note of appreciation by addressing specifically a person's actions and the impact they made on you and the organization. The best part – mail it to their home address! Building relationships through expression of genuine appreciation is priceless!

Melissa Wood, Alto, Texas

One thing truly effective leaders should do is give people **HOPE**. And leaders can do that by:

1. Helping them thrive
2. Openly praising accomplishments
3. Promoting positive growth, and
4. Embracing their value.

Lee Moreno, Tallahassee, Florida

30

The best leaders are ones who think **INTENTION FIRST**. Motivate your team by describing the intentions behind goals – the purpose, the action steps needed to reach the goals, what results you are working toward, and the attitudes necessary to get the end result. Your team will be more productive when they know the intention first.

Beth Camille Byram, Coto de Caza, California

Truly effective leaders do not complain. They take action to make a situation better.

Sharon A. Martin, Pittsburgh, Pennsylvania

I started my career out at the front desk of a primary care clinic and have worked my way up to management. I have always remembered how hard I worked and the pride I took in my daily duties with the main goal of wanting to feel appreciated or even noticed by my boss. There is a small, yet very effective way of communication that I use daily: I tell all my employees EVERY DAY when they are walking out the door, "Thank you!" I even try to put a specific situation in there for some employees if I know of something good that happened that day. I love to see the smile my comments put on my employees' faces!

Tina Fasone, Olathe, Kansas

Taking the time to "smell the roses" means more than an occasional break or a vacation. It's an attitude … a daily mindset that we, as leaders, must embrace. We sometimes get so focused on tasks and deadlines that we may lose our happiness factor. Don't think for one minute that employees won't recognize an uptight, stressed out, and generally "too serious" manager. Interacting with a manager or leader is much more palatable when it's coming from someone who demonstrates a sunny disposition.

When you think about it, personality, thoughts, and behaviors have the greatest impact on our lives, our well-being, and relationships with others. Employees want to work for a leader who is content and happy. Here are a few fundamental elements of a peaceful and effective leader:

- **Devoting time to family and friends**
- **Appreciating what they have**
- **Maintaining an optimistic outlook**
- **Feeling a sense of purpose**
- **Living in the moment**
- **Don't worry, be happy! :)**

Monica Kelly, Columbia, South Carolina

Hire for attitude, train for skills.

Sally Sandine, Waukegan, Illinois

Truly effective leaders *mine* the little things, and then *mind* the little things. They survey employees immediately after joining the organization to find out everything they can about their professional and personal interests. They ask questions like *What do you need in order to do your best work? What are your hobbies? What skills and passions do you bring to the team?* Then they use this information to assign special projects; select rewards and incentives, and build rapport with and among team members. They also notice small details, like who fixed the broken coffee maker or who helped clean up after the meeting, and acknowledge team members with a short thank you note left serendipitously in their work area. *Mining and minding* the little things lets employees know that you value them as individuals and shows them that you are aware of their contributions.

Stephanie Moss, Houston, Texas

Share the experience, whether good or bad! Every morning we have a 10-15-minute team huddle where we all share our "to-do's" for the day as well as the "ta-das." Since we are an IT department, we talk about what software changes will occur, if any, for that day; whom to call if there is a problem; any hardware issues everyone should know about; and any success/oops stories we have. We also talk about personal items we want to share – such as someone is going to be a grandmother, whose baby is walking, who got a new car, etc. Sharing at many levels helps to keep us a well-knit group and lets everyone know they are an important part of our team.

Sandra Osborne, RN, BSN, Charleroi, Pennsylvania

10 Reasons Why Leaders Should Keep Commitments and Model Positive Attitudes

1. It improves trust and respect at all levels.
2. It enhances leadership's reputation.
3. It increases team members' willingness to make and keep *their* commitments.
4. It eliminates inconsistencies that become obstacles to good team member attitudes.
5. It increases team members' cooperation with leadership.
6. It fosters a positive work culture.
7. It enhances customer service.
8. It increases pride, professionalism, and productivity.
9. It enhances the organization's ability to attract and retain high-quality and diverse team members.
10. It helps ensure the short AND long-term success of the enterprise.

And a Bonus Reason ...

11. It's purely and simply the right thing to do!

180 Ways to Build Commitment & Positive Attitudes
a walkthetalk.com publication

Truly effective leaders remember the special days of their team members. Birthdays, anniversaries, project completion dates, major accomplishments, etc., that matter to team members should all be remembered and celebrated. A simple note or email letting the person know you are thinking of them on their special day, glad they are part of the team, and wishing them future success, birthdays, etc., goes a long way. Team members feel valued and important to the success of the team.

Robin Smith, Saxton, Pennsylvania

Effective leaders always attack the problem and never the person. Every person has unique gifts and talents to bring to the table. Along with that, each one has the inherent desire to be acknowledged, accepted and appreciated. We all make occasional mistakes, and while it is important that our team members be accountable for their actions, it is even more important that we partner with them to help them understand the mistakes made, and support them as they work toward a positive resolution.

Carolyn Trana, Fargo, North Dakota

How to build a positive team spirit and working environment: Always start your day with a smile – lots of them. Regardless of how positive or negative things are when you start work, smiling helps the flow of positive thinking. It will set the tone, encourage trust among your peers and your team, and relieve potential stress if the first thing people see when you walk in is your smile.

Philly Teixeira, Marseille, France

Always believe that EVEN THE BEST CAN BE IMPROVED.

Shahid Sattar Awan, Karachi, Pakistan

Truly effective leaders acknowledge staff! At my workplace, we have an executive-level manager who always acknowledges staff members – regardless of whether they are cleaners (janitors) or peer executives … no matter if they are his direct reports or not. Every morning, he makes a quick lap around the workplace and says good morning to everyone. He also acknowledges staff who may be present when he wishes to talk to someone particular. He regularly updates everyone about workplace plans and decisions. He is well-respected, appreciated, and approachable. There is another executive manager who never speaks to staff, other than managers, unless he has to. He totally ignores other employees who may be present when he wishes to talk to someone in particular. As a result, he is perceived as being rude, ignorant, and unapproachable.

The small investment in time expressed by the first executive manager in always greeting people pays high dividends in cooperation, workplace harmony, and productivity. This gentleman is truly an effective manager.

Linda Brook-Franklin, Taree, NSW, Australia

In order to be an effective leader, you must understand how to address the personalities of your direct reports. You can't treat every personality the same and expect the same results. Is this psychology? In some ways, yes. But more importantly, it's the sign of a leader who can gain the respect of his/her employees and get the most positive outcomes for success. When giving instructions to a certain employee, it may be appropriate to say "I need you to take over a project for me and I need it completed immediately!" For another person, saying, "I have a project that could really use your expertise in order to meet our customer's deadline" may be a better match to his or her personality. Knowing what to say and how to say it – that's effective leadership!

Del McCall, PHR, Franklin Park, New Jersey

We often hear the phrase, "Begin with the end in mind." While that is important, good leaders know that too much attention to vision can be distracting. Rory McIlroy came into the final day of the 2011 Masters Golf Tournament with a lead and a chance for his first major win. Overwhelmed by the possibility, he played horribly and went off dejected rather than victorious. A few weeks later, in the U.S. Open, the scene was repeated. McIlroy came to the last day with a big lead. This time, however, he won easily. The difference? "It was only going to be hard if I made it hard. I felt as if I did a really good job of keeping myself right in the moment…" Good leaders help people see enough vision to be motivated. But they focus the work by fully engaging the present and helping people succeed at doing what needs doing now.

Dave Daubert, Elgin, Illinois

Remember the **E + R = O** formula. **E** equals any event that happens. You won't always have control over that event. **R** equals your reaction and response to the event. You always have control over how you react to an event. **O** equals the outcome. Whenever an **E**vent happens, how you **R**eact and respond (your choice) has a direct impact on the final **O**utcome.

Greg Carr, Frisco, Texas

People don't care how much you know until they know how much you care. The one thing you can do, around which all other idioms revolve, is to care about those on your team. When the leader exhibits this positive energy, the respect to you and for others will flow, self-confidence will build, the perseverance of team members will be present, action will take place, excuses will lessen, pride will show its face, and a cohesive family will blossom. The effective leader caring about his team will rub off on all members of the team in a positive fashion. This is the foundation of success which will perpetuate for generations.

Georgia Willis Fauber, Lynchburg, Virginia

Remember these two important words: **ATTITUDE** – Every day you have a choice whether to have a good attitude or a bad one. Choose to have the most positive attitude possible. **CHALLENGES** – Obstacles are merely challenging opportunities to do a better job at what you're doing on this day at this time. Everything that seems tough, today, is but a challenging opportunity.

Faith Shepard, Memphis, Tennessee

Driving High-
Quality Results

The person who gets the most satisfactory results is
not always the one with the most brilliant single mind,
but rather the one who can best coordinate
the brains and talents of his or her associates.

~ Alton W. Jones
(adaptation)

Truly effective leaders provide Strategic **D.I.R.E.C.T.I.O.N.** to the organization. They …

D irect strategic plan and actions

I nform stakeholders of expectations

R ally stakeholders toward common objectives

E xercise tremendous tenacity in dealing with others

C ommunicate! Communicate! Communicate!

T hank performers of the team on an ongoing basis

I nspire confidence in all followers

O pen their minds to new possibilities and ways of doing things

N ever fail to deliver on promises made.

Joseph N. Jacob, Port of Spain, Trinidad

Consider employees' time as important as your own. Don't waste your employee's time!

Donna Springs, Stanley, North Carolina

Hold quarterly performance discussions with all of your team members. Quarterly discussions allow for timely reviews of goals and objectives, adjustments are easier to make if necessary, and feedback is timed closer to actual events. You'll communicate better and you'll build trust with your staff because they feel you are invested in their success.

Dorothy Hall, Syracuse, New York

Effective leaders understand how their employees process and retain information. I use a "5,4,3,2,1 approach" that has improved my overall results tremendously. I work in a call center and my team of specialists takes insurance claims from across the country. We were struggling with compliance and quality assurance until I put this plan in place, and we are now number one in our office.

I send the same important information 5 times (i.e., daily) for a week in different formats: emails, banners, cards on their desk, notes written on bananas, etc. The following week, I send it 4 times, the third week, 3 times and so on. When I get down to 1, I send out the information once a week for a month. Afterwards, they can recall the information immediately – even in stressful situations. This has increased confidence in their abilities, and we have built those small successes into something more powerful.

Charlene Djurdjevic, Madison, Wisconsin

Leaders should have a vision – and share that vision in ways their teams can understand. Then make quarterly goals and monthly action plans together with the team. Let team members select what they will do (based on their talents and capacities) and set target dates for completing the jobs. Leaders should also ensure that performance is reviewed and discussed after completion and the key learning is made known to the entire team. Be sure to praise the good performers and encourage the others to learn and make new action plans for improving their own performance.

Annie Andrade, Mumbai, India

Leaders who are truly effective focus on what they DO want versus what they don't want. Ineffective leaders often talk about the problem, what limits getting to a goal, and worst of all, who's to blame. Sure, a leader needs to identify what the problem is, but effective leaders quickly redirect attention to: the desired outcome, the benefits of reaching that outcome, and the evidence of success. A focus on the outcome moves people toward positive success which is much more motivating than staying stuck in the problem discussion! For example, an effective leader I know gets her meetings back on track by asking subtly, "Ok, those statements are what we don't want. What is it we want to end up with today?" or "So now that we have clarity about what the problem is, what do we see as the desired outcome?" Try it yourself … it works!

Diane Dean, Austin, Texas

My philosophy is **YOU GET WHAT YOU INSPECT, NOT WHAT YOU EXPECT**. Be consistent in emphasizing the right way of doing things with constant follow-ups. Inspect things you trained your managers on and have them do the same with their team members. Don't just say, "I expect [or the position expects] these things from you." Inspect and follow up – you will get 100% from your team.

Akbar Rajani, Snellville, Georgia

Leadership Is About Making More

Some leaders believe that in order to achieve prosperity, they need to make more. And they're absolutely right! They do need to make more. YOU need to make more!

But that "more" cannot just be an increased salary or additional perks. Sure, those benefits would be nice – and we certainly wouldn't turn them down if offered. However, truly effective leaders understand that personal gain cannot be a singular objective. They understand that their organizations and teams, and they themselves, prosper when they focus on ensuring that …

More customers receive superior service;

More goals are set and achieved;

More skills are developed and honed by team members;

More opportunities for growth are created;

More obstacles to performance are minimized or eliminated;

More respect is demonstrated;

More communication and better listening take place;

More quality products and services are delivered;

More information is shared;

More successes are celebrated;

More responsibility is assumed;

More commitment and satisfaction are realized.

Effective leaders focus on these multiplier outcomes … and on, you guessed it, much *more*. Commit to following their lead.

The 10 Commandments of Leadership
a walkthetalk.com publication

Effective leaders communicate openly with their teams. Here are some examples:

- Conduct regular one-on-one meetings with direct reports. These meetings give both leader and team members the opportunity to discuss any topic openly and in private. These meetings should be conducted on a regular schedule.

- Set clear expectations. Leaders should clearly communicate what their expectations are in every situation and provide the necessary tools and resources to help the team members achieve the expectations and goals. When a team achieves goals, it builds confidence. A confident team truly is an unstoppable team.

- Conduct regular team meetings. Team meetings provide a setting where team members can interact with each other, issues can be discussed openly, the leader can get the same "message" out to all team members, and there is opportunity for further team building.

Christina Lurch, Allentown, Pennsylvania

We have our people write individual business plan goals each year. Then we meet with them quarterly to review their goals and results. We encourage them to reflect on what's working well and what things they need to do differently next quarter to achieve their goals. The plans are fluid documents – we revise them as needed. This helps team members to stay focused on their goals – which ultimately contributes to reaching our organizational goals.

P.J. Furnari, Clifton Park, New York

Express interest in each team member's success and personal well-being. Individual leader behavior is the single-most important predictor of organizational performance. Performance is a function of technical skill and behavior skill. Making a connection with people as a leader is a key behavior skill to help maximize individual and team performance. Legendary football coach Vince Lombardi, was a true master at making this emotional connection with each individual player. Make new members of your team feel welcome and help ease their transition to the team. Get to know your employees as people with lives outside of work. You will discover you have a lot more in common with one another. This shared commonality will help you build the connection that drives peak performance.

Dr. Michael E. Frisina, Columbia, South Carolina

I am reminded of the most important and often neglected skills all good leaders have – the ability to hire well. My experience is that truly effective leaders consistently hire future effective leaders – people who contribute immediately and, perhaps most importantly, fit the culture, atmosphere, and maturity required for the position at hand. Certainly a candidate must possess the requisite technical skills and background for a position. But when I look back at hiring decisions I have made, the difference between success and failure has rarely revolved around technical competence. Almost always it has rested with a candidate's fit into the organization. What is meant by "fit"? It is different for each organization, in fact, for each position. But strong leaders, aware of this important hiring criteria, know it when they see it.

Michael J. King, City of Industry, California

KEEP IT SIMPLE! Too often leaders miss the mark when presenting their message for the following reasons:

1. Providing too much detail.

Big ideas are buried in the presentation. Effective leaders make their big ideas stand out. They remove the clutter. They eliminate the things of little value to their message. Impactful communicators make their message concise – as long as necessary, as short as possible.

2. Not identifying actionable steps for people to take.

The best leaders describe one or more actionable steps people can take. If people are left with no specific actions to take, they typically keep doing what they have always done. It's business as usual.

3. Not convincing people to take action.

Impactful leaders make the sale. They present the facts, arguments, and emotional appeals that help convince people to take action. They explain what's in it for the audience and why it's important to act now.
In some cases, the leader needs to explain the negative consequences of not taking action. Effective presenters deliver their messages with great passion and conviction which helps seal the deal.

The challenge for all leaders is to:

- **Make their big ideas crystal clear;**
- **Identify actionable steps;**
- **Convince people it's the right thing to do.**

Paul B. Thornton, Chicopee, Massachusetts

Encouraging Innovation and Creativity

Innovation has nothing to do with how many R&D dollars you have … It's about the *people* you have, how you're led, and how much you get it.

~ *Steve Jobs*

Allow team members to fail! Just as Thomas Edison came up with 1,000 ways not to make a light bulb, not every idea or project ends in success. However, the ability for each employee to propose new ideas – without the fear of punishment if the proposal or design flops – creates an environment for a greater number of possibilities to be advanced. It then becomes the leader's responsibility to ensure that effective financial controls exist so the potential cost of failure does not exceed the business' ability to absorb the outlay.

Craig N. Cohen, St. Louis, Missouri

Be approachable. An employee should be able to walk into your office and tell you they just discovered a mistake they made and know you will jump in to HELP, not jump on them. Many mistakes can be corrected and be resolved quite easily if caught early – but not if they are covered up or swept under the rug.

Let your employees know the sooner they bring a problem to you, the better for the organization. Because, believe me, someday you will make a mistake and if you are lucky, your employee can bring it to you so you have the chance to make a quick correction. This takes trust. If team members are afraid of your temper or angry reaction, you will miss your opportunity.

Diana Merkel, Norfolk, Nebraska

The most highly effective and respected leaders get buy-in. How do they do it? By always explaining the why behind their request, and by allowing others to offer alternate approaches and solutions whenever possible!

Phil Gerbyshak, Milwaukee, Wisconsin

Effective leaders plan ahead, are open to new ideas and solutions, encourage continuous learning and development, support experimentation, and make it easy for people to explore new roles ... always with the goal in mind. Effective leaders keep the energy flowing, personally and visibly working toward the goal. They share success stories and give credit to those who contributed. Great leaders have the next goal ready and communicate it passionately while celebrating successes; they keep everyone involved and feeling they are part of something special.

Kathleen Koechling, Durham, North Carolina

Show your staff that you are willing to take risks in the interest of progress – and encourage them to do the same. Choosing a path of least resistance seldom gets you what you want or where you need to be. If you have a reasonably sound idea or an inspired motivation to implement a new procedure, policy, or practice, then do it. New ideas can be unpopular and meet with resistance. But taking the road less travelled not only demonstrates initiative and courage; it also may produce staggeringly positive results.

Carolyn Worthington, PhD, Asheville, North Carolina

Truly effective leaders should always ask their employees for input, suggestions, ideas, and feedback before making operational changes. The employees who actually do the work have the most first-hand knowledge. Soliciting and using some or all of their feedback will facilitate change acceleration, improve morale, and engage employees in innovative thinking.

Debra A. Conner, Sturbridge, Massachusetts

The best leaders incorporate new strategies and ideas in their own work and challenge their team members to do the same. If a new strategy or idea is less than successful, then share lessons learned and regroup. Lack of success is reviewed as a learning experience – not a failure. Failure is doing the same thing again and again with the same results. Effective leaders are BOLD and embrace change. So set the example for others by leading the way and daring to view situations as opportunities to learn and grow.

Kathryn Rhodes, Loudon, Tennessee

Delegate and have employees take responsibility for their assigned tasks. You must show confidence in the individual to whom you have delegated the task(s) by giving him or her the authority to make decisions related to that task without interference from you.

Patrick Gambin, McIvers, Newfoundland and Labrador

Motivation Tips to Encourage Involvement and Creativity

Teach Business Literacy. One powerful way to get employees motivated is to teach them the business of the business. The more people understand how a successful organization is run, the better they'll be able to contribute to your overall mission and the bottom line ... and feel like they truly are a part of your success.

Involve Them in Decision-Making. Have an important decision to make? Let employees decide! Or at least ask for their ideas and suggestions. They are, after all, the ones who will feel the impact the most. Besides, you'll probably end up with a better decision – one that your people will be inclined to support because they helped make it.

Let Your Employees Lead. Help others on your team develop by letting them take the lead on certain activities and projects. Most of us like "being in charge" – at least some of the time. It's a great way to build skills, commitment, and responsibility.

Keep Them Informed. Conduct regular "state of the business" meetings to keep everyone informed on what's happening within the organization (future plans, new products or services, planned purchases, etc.). Make sure people do NOT feel "kept in the dark."

Nuts 'n Bolts Leadership
a walkthetalk.com publication

The difference between an average leader and a great leader is, in a word, *flexibility*. Be willing to stretch your mind – allowing some "wiggle room" when brainstorming ideas – thereby acknowledging the strengths of those with whom you plan and progress.

While keeping the ultimate goal in sight, encourage creativity in the team. Even if ideas seem extreme at first, remember that outlandish suggestions – with a bit of modification – often springboard a project to new heights.

Set an example of flexibility by adjusting to new ideas and positive changes that enhance and improve the ultimate objective. Prepare for the unexpected so that unforeseen occurrences will merely challenge the group's resilience rather than impede the progress of the alliance.

Most importantly, applaud and support your team as together you leap through hoops, bend around obstacles, and bound to the finish line with results that surpass all expectations.

Martha Pendleton Jones, Great Falls, Montana

Think of **L.E.A.D.E.R.** as an acronym for Listen, Empower, Advocate, Develop, Encourage, and Role model.

Listen to customers and employees regarding their needs and challenges. Communicate with them on both strategic and functional issues – why we do and what we do.

Empower employees to make decisions affecting them and their customers.

Advocate and drive business excellence through engagement opportunities in committees, task forces, teams, etc. Commit resources, money, and people to the mission and goals.

Develop and coach employees to enhance their competencies through training, tutoring (one-to-one), and coaching.

Encourage and motivate employees to do better for themselves and their customers. Recognize their achievements through compensation, recognition and rewards. Celebrate success.

Role model – be an example of walking the talk.

Johnson Ong, Singapore, Republic of Singapore

Leaders should be willing to accept that not everyone thinks as they do, looks as they do, or acts as they do. Diversity not only means race or ethnicity; it means having visible and invisible disabilities, sexual orientation, gender identity, cultural differences, and diversity of thought. The truly effective leader recognizes and values each and every employee because of the unique talent he or she brings to the team.

Leaders should welcome all employees to the workplace and provide them with a mentor/buddy for the first six months of their employment. Job hunting today is so stressful and leaders should provide a positive welcoming experience to new hires.

Fredda Shere-Valenti, Rockville, Maryland

"Hold Your Tongue." Let your team of employees know what is expected of them on a particular task – including the date and time the task should be completed. Encourage them to let you know if they have any questions or need any type of assistance, then …

LEAVE THEM ALONE!

Let them work out their own mistakes – don't solve problems for them. Give high praise when the task is completed correctly. They will be full of pride on their great accomplishments, and they will know that you trust their abilities.

Marla Kapner, West Caldwell, New Jersey

Responsibility: Taking It and Giving It

In the final analysis, the one quality that all successful people have is the ability to take on responsibility.

~ Michael Korda

Conduct honest conversations immediately to address any undesired behaviors that you observe. These conversations can be challenging, so try using this really effective model to help you give quick, honest 60-second feedback and remain in control – it's called *DESC:*

D - Describe the situation (what you have observed)
E - Explain how this makes you feel (frustrated, disappointed, etc.)
S - Specifics (facts)
C - Consequences (what will happen if this behavior continues).

Note: Discussing consequences often is more powerful when asked like this: *What do you think will happen if this behavior continues?* Most employees will give you the worst-case scenario – one probably far worse than any consequence you had in mind. This will give you the option to then coach them away from that consequence toward more effective behaviors and a positive outcome.

Craig Timmins, Livingston, Scotland

Effective and respected leaders take responsibility for the actions and work of their team. When it comes to work performance and behavior, the good, the bad, and the ugly ultimately are all your responsibility. If individuals on your team misstep, they need to know that you will work with them to make any necessary adjustments and move on – not complain about them to others.

Debra Newman, Toronto, Ontario

Keep it simple! Clear direction. Defined goals. Proper tools. Appropriate staffing. Get out of their way! REPEAT!

Ken E. Roy, Vista, California

Effective leaders should listen and encourage participation and responsibility. They should promote group work to increase the number of participants. They should assign observational exercises to determine each person's level of perception. They should commend where necessary and be forthright with corrections. Leaders should support individual thinking and introduce new ideas to expand each team member's thought processes. They should prepare people to take on more by giving challenging assignments and reversing roles to promote confidence and advanced thinking. They should teach, model, and promote effective listening. They should reward initiative. Finally, they should just be there as a support for everyone.

Camille C. Bullard, Nassau, The Bahamas

Do not allow the "I thought" of inefficiency. "I thought" is the most often given excuse why goals are not met, reports are not on time, schedules are not kept, and directions are not followed:

I thought it was taken care of.
I thought someone else was going to do it.
I thought it was not due until next week.

Effective leaders do not tolerate "I thought." They require results like:

I have taken care of it.
I have completed the assignment on time.

They eliminate this crutch of inefficiency through clear communication and expectations: They check to make sure people understand what is to be done and by when. They verify. They follow up. They remain accessible for clarification.

David T. Perry, Milledgeville, Georgia

THE "O" WORD

If there's any concept that's synonymous with leadership, it's got to be responsibility. And, behaviorally, that translates into

OWNERSHIP.

To be an effective and respected leader ...

... You must **own** (i.e., support and be committed to) your organization's mission, plans, and initiatives.

... You must **own** all of the duties and responsibilities that come with your job.

... You must **own** (i.e., be accountable for) the performance and results of your team.

... You must **own** (i.e., admit to and fix) your personal mistakes and shortcomings.

LEAD RIGHT
a walkthetalk.com publication

My motto is: My successes are mine and my failures are mine. I own it. We all need to take responsibility for our own actions. Stop blaming the person who sponsored you. You will only succeed if you put the work in. Others can't do it for you. So many times people want things handed to them. The old saying still applies: "If it is worth having, it is worth working for."

Sandy Kroese, Powder Springs, Georgia

Be an effective and responsible leader by making decisions in a timely manner. Do not struggle and wait until it is too late and the deadline passes; This is frustrating for the team of employees who spent hours putting the project together. Communicate with all team members and consider their feedback – including opposing views. Then, move forward and resolve issues by making a final determination in a timely manner.

Ann DiTroia, Garden City, New York

Effective leaders should hold their employees accountable with achievable goals. When a team member completes something you have asked of them (no matter how small the task), reward them with a thank you card or some other form of recognition. Your staff needs to feel appreciated. As you recognize small achievements, you gain support and buy-in as you have larger tasks to complete. Likewise, if they are not fulfilling their tasks or goals, coaching and mentoring them are crucial. Ask, (in a non-threatening manner) how you can help them to succeed.

Jill Hopper, Boise, Idaho

The best thing a leader can do for someone looking to grow is provide them ownership and the responsibilities of a task or stretch opportunity that will help them obtain the skills they are looking for.

Willie Ryder, Charlotte, North Carolina

Leaders should admit when they make mistakes.

Leslie Clark, Keizer, Oregon

Effective leaders recognize the need to be accountable for the individuals who are part of their teams. Often the foundation of trust and respect is built upon the critical platform of follow-through. Strong follow-up on ideas, feedback, and professional development requests is of paramount importance. Take time to identify areas of specific needs for individuals as well as for the entire group you lead. Strive to not over-promise and under-deliver. Choose two to three action items and take team ownership of them. Work to make changes/improvements happen as quickly as possible. If you follow through effectively, they will follow you!

Patrick Sullivan, Wilmington, North Carolina

A truly effective leader desires to lead by serving others. Allow others to observe basic and mundane tasks that you graciously and quietly complete without any expectation of receiving a pat on the back or a "way to go." Be caught cheerfully picking up trash from the customer and employee parking lots, cleaning the break room, tidying up after an employee party or meeting, straightening lobby areas, or pitching in with answering phones on an exceptionally busy day.

Karen Diane Sims, Whitehouse, Texas

Serving with Passion

You really can change the world if you care enough.

~ *Marion Wright Edelman*

Truly effective leaders are passionate about what they do. They live their lives devoted to the mission of the organization and to the needs of their team. They lead by example at all times. They are authentic in their communications. Feedback is honest, frequent, and balanced. It flows freely in all directions. Effective leaders willingly accept feedback on how they are doing and act on constructive advice. These leaders view people as integral to the success of the organization and as valued members of their team.

Geralyn Cappelli, New York, New York

Effective leaders in business, government, not-for-profits, and the military – whether or not they hold positions of authority – strive methodically to aim actions and thoughts toward serving others. One can begin with the threshold question: Who am I serving? Then, in all your interactions, ask: How can I best serve? Whether it's an interaction with a customer, a discussion with an employee, or just making a kind gesture to a stranger who has no foreseeable way to advance your interests, focusing on serving others can occasion a cascade of small steps – creating momentum toward an extraordinary leadership journey. [from *Serve to Lead*]

James M. Strock, Scottsdale, Arizona

The best leaders are passionate about their ideas. When the head of an organization truly believes in the direction she/he is taking the team, others will follow. In the same way that press begets more press, enthusiasm results in more enthusiasm. The most successful brands are those infused with passion, and that comes from the top down.

Lisa Hammond, Las Vegas, Nevada

Leaders should serve others with strength and compassion – two traits that go hand-in-hand. A strong leader is not iron-fisted but remains in control regardless of the situation. Whether he or she is the President of the United States or the director of a department, staff look to the leader to be the example. The leader does not have the luxury of falling apart. Compassion and caring about others are also necessary as leaders are dealing with human beings, not robots.

My department recently experienced a devastating incident that demanded I be strong and caring. A young home care RN was killed on duty in a car accident. I had to remain strong (despite my own sadness) in order to lead the team through this tragedy, yet be caring and assist them emotionally through the death of their coworker and friend. These were people suffering a horrible loss who needed my strength to hold them up – as well as my compassion to help them through.

Barbara Keough, RN, MGS, Dubuque, Iowa

Feelings are not right nor are they wrong. They just ARE! When managing a team, I have found that it's important to recall this adage when members express great passion for an idea. It empowers me to listen actively without exercising judgment, glean the "pearl" or authentic truth of what is being said, and then react appropriately. Following this advice allows me to understand and respond to the idea behind expressed emotions rather than be distracted by the emotion itself. Doing so builds trust and empathy among all team members – creating a fertile environment for idea sharing and brainstorming.

Kristin Dillon Webb, Glen Mills, Pennsylvania

Here are four ways leaders can serve those they lead:

1. *Motivate team members by offering something different every so often, like a workshop or a team-building activity.*

2. **Allow them to grow through training and special assignments.**

3. *Be a good example in the everyday routine. If you require the team to be punctual, be punctual yourself. If you want to be respected, show respect for all team members.*

4. *Speak highly of them, and in situations where they commit a service failure, discuss what went wrong in the process. Focus on the process instead of the person.*

Maria Loreto Sevilla-Manalansan, Pasay City, Philippines

Truly effective leaders honor and serve the most important assets in business: the staff. How? By catching them doing things right. Management by walking around is a known success strategy. An employer who is visible on the work floor – be it in an office or a plant – and acknowledges behaviors he or she encourages will get more of the same. Being visible at the end of the work day is also a valuable role-modeling behavior.

Helene Bulger, Winnipeg, Manitoba

When your focus is on service, in whatever it is you are passionate about, you will be successful.

Donna M. Bucher, Bradenton, Florida

64

Truly effective leaders are **PASSIONATE.** It doesn't matter if you are leading a meeting about changes to office workflow, explaining to your staff how budgetary processes work, or celebrating a team success; you must be passionate and enthusiastic about your topic. After all, if you barely care, why should they?

Jeff Stewart, Hopkinsville, Kentucky

A leader must define *purpose* for the team. With a well-defined and well-communicated sense of purpose, teams know what they "own." Team members are motivated and feel they can be more creative in their contributions. With purpose come results – without purpose comes conflict. Can everyone on your team answer the question: *What is your purpose of this organization*? From that purpose will flow goals, dreams, desires, creativity, self-worth, and feelings of value.

David Davis, Sylvania, Ohio

Leaders love the people they serve. You will not always like everyone the same, but you must love them all. Leadership love is not about how you feel about those you serve, but about how you treat them. Live *"The Platinum Rule"* which states: *Treat others better than they treat you.* When it comes to how you treat others, being a leader is not about being right, but about doing right. It's about thinking the right thoughts, making the right choices, engaging in the right actions, saying the right words at the right time in the right tone, creating the right environment, treating others the right way, speaking up and defending what is right.

Steve Schultz, Fountain Valley, California

5 Ways to Demonstrate
Leadership Passion

1. *Think of each member of your work group as a high jumper.*
   Celebrate the reaching of new heights – then "raise the bar," together. But don't forget, as you're raising that bar, so is your competition.

2. *Learn by teaching.* Volunteer to be an instructor for organizational
   training programs. You'll not only develop in-depth knowledge about
   subjects you prepare to teach; you'll also be able to help others
   develop and grow.

3. *Get excited about positive things.* If you're normally calm and
   reserved, pick something you're "fired-up" about and act yourself
   into excitement. Initiate enthusiasm and the feeling will follow!

4. *Spread the sparkle.* Get enthused about coworkers who are
   enthusiastic – it's contagious and can snowball very quickly.
   Recognize and reward those who help contribute to a culture
   of contagious enthusiasm.

5. *Regularly spend one-on-one time with each member of your
   team.* Open these informal get-togethers with a general question
   like: *How are things going with you?* Then really listen to what
   they have to say. Listening is an important way to demonstrate
   that you care.

144 Ways to Walk the Talk
a walkthetalk.com publication

Helping Others Succeed

A leader's role is to raise people's aspirations
for what they can become, and to release
their energies so they will try to get there.

~ *David R. Gergen*

An effective leader creates an environment where people WANT to stand in their absolute best light. When creating happy workers, productivity knows no bounds! People who want to make good things happen because they are so excited and feel so great about their own role in doing it will produce results beyond predictions. Every day, that leader needs to let his or her employees know how valuable they are – through words of praise and thanks such as: Great job on the last contract … Wonderful idea for the housekeeping problem - and most importantly – *I could not do this without you. You are a vital member of our team.*

Then follow up by giving credit at a meeting to someone who went "above and beyond." Do NOT be a glory hog or pat yourself on the back – that is sad and pathetic. Give praise frequently – even for the small things. Give praise in public among others, but give constructive criticism in private – absolutely NEVER where others can hear. Create an employee of the month board, a birthday club, or a day where the whole staff chooses one member to honor by putting little notes of appreciation in their e-box or mailbox. The choices are limitless on how to show appreciation and recognition.

Ellen Dragonetti, Fontana, Wisconsin

Truly effective leaders develop their team members both personally and professionally by setting the example as well as providing tools for improvement such as books, magazines, blogs, newsletters, mentorship, and helping them learn from their mistakes. Being honest and approachable is the key!

Kelli Matheny, Seattle, Washington

I have four principles that I share with the staff in our facility:

1. *Show up for work on time.*
2. *Do your job as best you can.*
3. *Respect the clients (or the customer).*
4. *Respect each other.*

What I can tell you is that if these four principles are followed, people work effectively. If we are having trouble, it is likely because of an infringement of one of these four principles!

Mary Ellen Parsons, Swan River, Manitoba

One thing that truly effective leaders do is recognize the value that other people add. You can recognize great leaders by how well they listen and what questions they ask. They see beyond the immediate and they ask questions in a way that does not minimize nor discount what they are hearing. They make the other person, however big or small their credentials, feel that what they have to say is truly important and the spirit of what they are saying is being heard and is given thoughtful consideration.

Deborah Deivasigamani, Evanston, Illinois

Let go of feedback and learn how to feed forward – as in "Here's what you can try next time." It is a coaching tool that reinforces expectations of the positive behavior from here forward – changing the focus from the negative connotation related to reviewing the past and what went wrong. Leaders cannot go back and change history, but we can have a positive influence on staff and their future behaviors.

Jan M. McKeown, Great Falls, Montana

Don't just be a good listener, be a reactive listener. Stop whatever you're doing and give people your total attention, make eye contact, and avoid interrupting them before they stop speaking. Those certainly are all good things to do. But once you have done all of that, if it's in your power to affect a change or provide assistance, be reactive to the situation and do something positive that truly proves you were listening. Simply paying attention and using body language to show you were listening is not enough. You must also demonstrate – by your actions afterwards – that their concerns are now your concerns. If you are in a leadership position and have the power to change something, make it happen.

Vernita Dorsey, New Castle, Delaware

Share the vision. Nothing is less interesting than riding on a bus to "who knows where or why." Tell your team where you want to go and why, and ask how each might contribute to the journey. Then stand back and watch the world unfold before your eyes.

Katie Seifert, Spring, Texas

A great leader knows that each employee has something unique to contribute and values the differences that each one brings to the team. Instead of focusing on employee shortfalls, a great leader is skilled at finding what employees "do well" and encourages those individuals to build on their strengths. The great leader always credits the team with successes – which creates more momentum, as employees who feel appreciated are much more satisfied with their work environment.

Sherri Gerek, Columbia Falls, Montana

Take time to get all the facts before drawing any conclusions. Learn to improve together by identifying who the key players involved are and asking open-ended questions for their input on the situation at hand. Validate the facts and then ask, *What could we/you do better the next time to get a better result?*

Deborah J Thiel, RD, MPH, Tomah, Wisconsin

Truly effective leaders help their team members succeed by providing feedback which is:

- ***Timely*** – Effective leaders do not wait for a year-end review to reward or reprimand behavior; they fully understand that feedback is most powerful when it's immediate.

- ***Private*** – Although leaders may choose to praise in public, correcting discussions should always be in private.

- ***Specific and to the point*** – Effective leaders do not waste their time or employee's time; when providing feedback, they quickly get to the heart of the matter.

- ***Consistent*** – Effective leaders are consistent in the way they deliver feedback, both in speech and action.

- ***Inspiring*** – Effective leaders use feedback to inspire poor performers to change course and rocket super stars to higher performance.

Laurence A. Pitcaithly, Houston, Texas

Self-Reflection Questions

In the last several months, what have I done to ...

... Be accessible (physically and mentally) to employees who would like my attention?

... Be considerate of team member needs?

... Provide employees with the training, tools, resources, and feedback required for success?

... Keep employees in the "what's happening" information loop?

... Help team members maintain an appropriate balance between their professional and personal lives?

... Demonstrate respect for employees' time and talents – as well as respect for them as individuals?

... Solicit, and listen to, team members' ideas and concerns?

... Help everyone develop and grow?

... Fairly distribute the work and workload?

The Leadership Secrets of Santa Claus
a walkthetalk.com publication

Address conflicts that hamper success. When a conflict arises it's always important to stay calm and take a neutral stance. Keep your emotions out of it; don't jump to conclusions. Get everyone's "story" individually, and ask how they would propose the problem be fixed. Once you have compiled and analyzed all of the necessary data, come up with a solution. Mediate/counsel the involved parties as necessary.

Cindy Strigel, Milwaukee, Wisconsin

Truly effective leaders must always be prepared for the inevitable. Things will not always go as planned. When the train goes (or appears to go) off the rails, an effective leader will "hit the ground running" to find the right solution. In doing so, he or she will look at all areas and people concerned objectively, without bias. In the process of finding the solution, an effective leader will be gracious enough to acknowledge that he/she is as much to blame as anyone else for what has happened – for not having foreseen something like that coming – and will not heap all the blame on the rest of the team. After a proper solution is found, an effective leader will review it over and over again with the team to make sure it is foolproof.

Mulwa Sadat, Nairobi, Kenya

Truly effective leaders talk to people the way they want to be talked to themselves. It's "The Golden Rule" applied to communication. Remove the emotion from the communication to keep the trust you have worked so hard to build. Do not scold employees – that only raises their defenses. Help them understand why their action(s) were undesirable and how to handle the situation if it comes up again.

Matt Dunivan, North Webster, Indiana

Effective leaders know when it's okay to jump in and get their hands dirty and when they need to stand back and just observe. It's never a good idea to do one or the other all the time. Effective leaders understand their employees' needs. There are times when people need their manager to show that they are not above giving a helping hand. There are other times when team members just need their manager to step back and allow them to figure it out on their own. A truly effective leader understands when to do both. The hands-on allows you to work together and coach along the way. Standing back and observing allows you to coach on achievements and opportunities.

Jason Mueller, Norman, Oklahoma

The greatest leaders are always looking to help develop others. They make themselves available to those wishing to grow and improve. They answer questions honestly and provide advice when appropriate; they are a welcome source of support and encouragement to those who need it. They share what they know and openly offer the experiences gained from their past successes and failures in order to help others learn. They give their time, knowledge, and support for nothing more than the opportunity to lift someone else up and help them on their journey to becoming the person they are meant to be.

Willie Ryder, Charlotte, North Carolina

Truly effective leaders invest time in developing other effective leaders. A manager should work with not only their supervisor and team leads but the general staff as well. They need to recognize the talents in each person and nurture them.

Kit Gontarek, Minneapolis, Minnesota

Inspiring Ethics
and Integrity

Real integrity is doing the right thing,
knowing that nobody's going to know whether
you did it or not.

~ Oprah Winfrey

A leader – whether he/she knows it, likes it, or wants to – shapes the perceptions others (both internal and external) have about the organization. Good or bad, people's perceptions of organizations are greatly impacted by behaviors, attitudes, and characters of the leadership. As a result, it is essential that all leaders represent their organizations well 24/7, 365 days a year by modeling excellence, high standards of ethics, and dedication. Leaders can do this by:

1. *Paying attention to what they say and how they act,*
2. *Soliciting honest feedback from all stakeholders,*
3. *Not using "power" or authority to take advantage of situations or people,*
4. *Following up on commitments made,*
5. *Reducing/eliminating gaps between words and actions,*
6. *Developing and maintaining positive relationships, and*
7. *Reducing, to the extent possible, personal ego.*

Daryl J. Delabbio, PhD., Rockford, Michigan

Truly effective leaders give people the "why" behind changes. They weigh options, suggestions, and facts before determining new directions. When a change is announced, they explain the thought process behind it so people won't make up their own version of why a decision was made – especially if it is an unpopular change. It's on the leader to really study the facts and make sure the decision is the best option for the situation and not just the way the leader wants it to be.

T. Gretz, Powell, Ohio

Never make a promise you cannot keep. You will truly kill your authority by this lethal mistake.

Cindy Kocher, Allentown, Pennsylvania

If an employee requests something, no matter how simple it might be, make sure you write the request down in front of the person. When you complete the request, return to the employee to let him/her know that you have addressed their request and what specifically was done. Requests represent employee concerns and therefore deserve your attention! Each request provides a great opportunity for you as a leader to show and reinforce empathy, awareness, loyalty, trust, feedback, honor, and character – in one simple act.

Martha Kaiser, Shelbyville, Tennessee

Do more than just talk a good game. Deliver! Empty promises and hypocrisy are two of the biggest enemies of trust. Leaders need to "walk the talk." When trust is genuine and followers feel supported and appreciated – genuinely, the power of a team is exponentially more than the sum of its parts.

Destine D. Holmgreen, Laredo, Texas

Leave your footprint – just make sure you're not stepping on people to do so.

Monica Kelly, Columbia, South Carolina

Effective leaders demonstrate ethics as a FIRST priority! They ensure that the basis of everyday business (the organization's mission, values statement, etc.) are tied to and governed by ethics. To ensure ethics is a first priority, effective leaders ask up front and out loud the tough questions that assemble ethical outcomes for everyday actions and decisions. I like to say, "Ethics keeps the good things good!"

Deb Miller, Freeland, Michigan

Write it down! I know it sounds incredibly simple, but it gets results. Keep a calendar or journal with lots of space for writing down your ideas, appointments, and goals. It's so much easier to make sure you follow through on a project when you can see it all on paper. Tracking how you are meeting your goals, making your ideas into reality, and staying on top of your schedule helps promote individual success and ethical behavior!

Jenny Whiteman, New Hope, Pennsylvania

Follow up on requests received from your staff within 24 – 48 hours. Even if you can't complete the request within that time frame, just saying you're working on it and can have it back to them by a certain time is so helpful. Otherwise, it may seem that a request has fallen into the black hole – never to be seen again — and leaving others wondering if you ever received it: *Are you just ignoring it? Should I proceed without hearing back from you?*

Marie Worrell, Mankato, Minnesota

CHECK BEFORE YOU ACT!

Check decisions and planned activities for "rightness" before implementing them. Use the questions below (or similar ones supplied by your organization) as your litmus test.

Answering "no" to one or more of the following would suggest the need to either develop an alternative strategy or to seek counsel and advice from appropriate sources:

THE ETHICAL ACTION TEST

A. **Is it legal?**

B. **Does it comply with our rules and guidelines?**

C. **Is it in sync with our organizational values?**

D. **Will I be comfortable and guilt-free if I do it?**

E. **Does it match our stated commitments and guarantees?**

F. **Would I do it to my family or friends?**

G. **Would I be perfectly okay with someone doing it to me?**

H. **Would the most ethical person I know do it?**

Ethics4Everyone
a walkthetalk.com publication

More important than anything else, being honest and truthful is one of the quickest paths to respect and effectiveness. And I don't mean just telling people you will be honest and truthful. More and more today, people "tell us" what they will do but then fail to deliver on what they are saying. Whenever I am dealing with anyone - on my team, in my business, or with suppliers or customers – I not only listen to what they say; I also watch what they do. It takes only one lie for a person's credibility to forever remain in question. In cases where the lie is clearly malicious -- one intended either to deceive or to avoid accountability – that person's value to me and to my business is lost forever.

Stephen G. Largy, Toronto, Ontario

Leaders will receive advice from a host of different people at different times. However, deep down, most leaders have an inner instinct as to what it is right and what is wrong. It is built up over years of experience – gaining advice from others and then formulating it into a sixth sense. Like everything else in the world, leadership evolves. Some advice will last you forever. Some advice will be useful at certain times or will change just as you, the role, and the world itself changes. While some pieces of advice are foolproof, others can be taken or left. You must find your own style and develop a sixth sense.

Neil McLennan, Edinburgh, Scotland

Effective leaders are upfront with their communication at the individual, team, and organizational levels regardless of how tough the message is.

Liz Johnson, Minneapolis, Minnesota

Truly effective leaders avoid playing the "I need to supply all the answers" game. In an economy defined by fierce competition and little reward, many employees are taking note of their bosses' actions. When a senior manager/boss is asked a question by another senior manager, and they don't have the answer but know that someone on their team does, rather than fetching the information themselves and reporting back, they should simply refer the senior manager to that team member. This does three things: **1.** It shows confidence in the member(s) of your team. **2.** It saves everyone a lot of time. **3.** It allows your team member(s) an opportunity to be recognized for their insight/ knowledge by other leaders.

Jose B. Boix, Pembroke Pines, Florida

Leading people is a privilege that needs to be earned – every day. Everyone has something to offer, and great leaders help bring out the best in the people they lead. They do this by building trust. The more you demonstrate trust in the people you lead, the more they will trust you. Make sure that every interaction you have with someone you lead improves the level of trust that person has in you. Deliver on your commitments. Let the people you lead know if you can't deliver on a commitment – right away. Give credit where it is due. Everyone likes to work for a leader who shares the credit for a job well done. Finally, we all make mistakes. Own up to yours. You'll become known as a straight shooter, honest with yourself and others, and, more important, worthy of the privilege of leading people.

Bud Bilanich, Denver, Colorado

As a leader, when you think of the word "control," you must reference this to yourself and not controlling those who work for or with you. Control is about being in control of how you do things like train, treat with fairness, and offer resources for success. It's about under-standing that accountability starts with you because you're the common denominator for each and every person who works with you. The control you have is over YOU! How you control *yourself* will influence how those whom you work with control *themselves*!

Andrae Chisolm, McDonough, Georgia

When things begin to go poorly, an effective leader will look within and honestly examine his/her own behavior and actions in order to determine how they are contributing to the problem before casting blame on others.

Scott E. Schoenberger, Chambersburg, Pennsylvania

1. Always speak the truth – then you don't have to remember to lie.
2. Be positive – it's contagious.
3. Believe in yourself and your goals – you'll maintain a healthy mind.
4. Maintain humility and respect for all – people remember how you make them feel.

Mari Matthew, Port of Spain, Trinidad

Practicing What You Preach

Example is not the main thing in influencing others. It is the ONLY thing.

~ Albert Schweitzer

Be consistent with the application of policies, standards, and rules. Do not give preferential treatment to one or two employees and expect the remaining team members to be accepting. This creates resentment toward not only the leader but toward the "privileged" employees as well. Everyone is working at the same organization and everyone must be held accountable for their actions. Example: Don't allow two employees to arrive for work late every day and reprimand – via dialog or annual review – the others. We all have things in our lives that we could use as excuses for being late, but most people are mature enough to know they should respect their positions enough to get there on time daily.

Melissa J. Williams, Jacksonville, Florida

Lead by example. Let your employees see you "roll up your sleeves" and do the job you expect them to do.

Kathy Turek, RN, Kenosha, Wisconsin

Effective leaders do what they say they are going to do. And before they can say what they are going to do, they listen and observe. When they see something that isn't working, they ask themselves, *How can this be fixed*? They do not blame their team. Effective leaders know that everything that goes wrong serves to teach them something. Once a problem or issue is clearly defined, effective leaders confront it head-on. They have the conversations that ineffective leaders are too afraid to have. They are passionate about self-growth and helping others – and expect the same from each team member. Effective leaders are relentless communicators who celebrate successes with the team that created them and learn from their losses.

Doreen Zayer, Staten Island, New York

Reveal all information that is pertinent to people doing their jobs. One of the worst feelings I have is when I am surprised by information I hear from the field that my superiors have revealed in a meeting but haven't told their own staffs. For example, a pending upgrade version of a product is incredible and exciting inside information. To find out that information from a customer is embarrassing, to say the least. Be truthful with information. Covering or hiding information that eventually leaks out is indeed frustrating. It makes it appear to my accounts that I am not on top of what is happening at my own company. Leaders need to trust their employees not to reveal company secrets.

Jeff Johnson, Omaha, Nebraska

Lead by example, not by words. Effective leaders do not ask others to do things that they would not be willing to do – or have not done in the past. If they are asking team members to make a significant change to their routine or workload, leaders should provide the tools and the support necessary to make the transition. If they are requesting a change in an employee's behavior, they should create an example of the behavior for the person to emulate. By leading in this manner, they gain the respect of their associates and create a bond of trust within the team. Leaders cannot be successful unless they have walked in the shoes of those who follow them and have created a safe path for them to follow on.

Melanie Wood, Centralia, Missouri

Leaders should be role models of their personal values and the organization's values. The following quote represents this: "A leader leads by example, whether he intends to or not" (*author unknown*). Leaders are constantly being watched. What they show and model will be viewed as important by their team. An organization's values can hang on a wall and lack a cultural impact because the leaders are not modeling behaviors that reflect the core values. In today's world, it is important for an organization to differentiate itself; an effective way to do this is to have strong values that are understood and reflected by all employees. Leaders must show the way by modeling the values and holding themselves and others accountable for doing the same.

Roberta L. Frizzell, Phoenixville, Pennsylvania

Always be time sensitive. If you are late to meetings with clients, subordinates, or your own managers, you show complete disrespect for everybody. By being late enough times you show your subordinates that your time is valuable only to you. Once you are considered habitually late, nobody will even try to be on time for you.

Mike Shea, Allentown, Pennsylvania

When you make a mistake, 'fess up immediately and fix it. We all have to deal with egos (including our own) every day. To be able to step back, admit your mistake, and then step up by correcting the problem demonstrates that you are human, you are humble, and you have integrity. You will be amazed at the reaction subordinates will have when you show them that "the boss" is a person too. After all, wouldn't you want your employees to do the same?

Jeff Stewart, Hopkinsville, Kentucky

Effective leaders model organizational values in all work environments. Start by taking a moment to write down four key beliefs and then monitor how you are living those beliefs in all settings for the next 24 hours. Be honest with yourself. Are your speech and temperament congruent with your customer service expectations for employees? Effective leaders don't miss an opportunity to lead by example. For me as a teacher, this means that while I'm in the school cafeteria, I am the first one to grab a mop if there's a spill (servant leadership). I'm engaging students with questions about their efforts in class (student learning). I'm positive and approachable to parents and staff (two-way communication). The language I use in spoken and written communication is synergistic with our team's goals (continuous improvement). Don't miss a single opportunity to walk the talk!

Brad Gustafson, Wayzata, Minnesota

Lead by example! Regardless of whether you are leading a family, leading factory workers, leading a group of teachers, etc., it is critical to lead by example. Actions speak louder than words. If you want others to be on time, then you must be on time – every time! If you want others to treat people with respect, then you must treat people with respect – always! If you expect people to produce, then you must produce – regularly! Celebrate the actions you desire and demonstrate on a regular basis. Too often, leaders forget what it was like to be led. Once they climb into that driver's chair, they forget what it was like to be in the back seat (or in the trunk!). Maintaining communication and a connection with workers is crucial to effective leadership. One way to lead is to make your performance the example you want team members to aspire to. Be the leader … by doing!

Dennis M. Docheff, Warrensburg, Missouri

3 IMPORTANT WAYS TO EARN EMPLOYEE **TRUST**

1. **Keep your promises.** You don't have to promise things just to make employees feel good. They're more interested in being able to depend on what you promise than in feeling good. Just keep the promises you do make and people will trust what you say.

2. **Speak out for what you think is important.** Team members can't read your mind. They don't always know what you're thinking. If they are guessing how you feel about something, they may guess wrong ... and act accordingly. Save them the trouble. Tell them what you feel is important – and why. They will respect you so much more.

3. **Do what you say you are going to do.** Just let your "yes" be "yes" and your "no" mean "no." When you tell employees that you're going to do something, they should be able to consider it done.

Listen Up, Leader!
a walkthetalk.com publication

One thing that truly effective leaders do is get in "the trenches" with their team. By performing various duties/responsibilities alongside your team, you are truly leading by example and giving everyone on the team the chance to get caught doing things RIGHT. Doing so helps to establish respect – not just as a leader, but a TEAM leader.

Lee Wrigley, Grande Prairie, Alberta

CLOSING THOUGHTS

Having a leadership position and actually being an effective and respected leader are not necessarily the same thing. Your position is something that was given to you – something you probably became eligible for by being a solid performer earlier in your career. What you did "yesterday," as an employee, helped you get the title/classification you hold today. And that's exactly what your position is: a title … a classification.

Being a true leader, however, is different. "Leader" is a label that you EARN through specific actions and behaviors. It's based on what you do today and tomorrow – not what's printed on your business cards, engraved on your name tag, or noted on your correspondence. Fact is, in order to be a true leader, you must DO the things that effective and respected leaders do. And identifying what many of those "things" are is what this book is all about.

Information that helps you improve your performance and enhance your success is truly a gift.

Now, you have been given 145 such gifts from contributors to this powerful resource. The big question that only you can answer: *What will you do with those gifts?* You can ignore them by stashing this book in a desk drawer or a rarely accessed bookshelf, or you can use them to maximize your leadership potential – and share them with others to help your colleagues do the same. Hopefully it's the latter two that you will choose. You owe that to yourself, your organization, and especially the people who depend on you so much.

Remember that the information found in *Hey Leader* represents the experience-based thoughts and perceptions of people just like you – and like those you lead. But as presented, they are just words … only good ideas. You have to put them into ACTION in order for their value and potential benefits to be realized. Only you can make that happen.

As you were reading, you undoubtedly came across many strategies and leadership behaviors that you already practice. Keep doing them! And for those that are not part of your normal routine – give them a try!
Both will serve you well.

You know, next to our hearts, our most valuable body parts as leaders are our ears. We need to listen to people's ideas, feelings, concerns – and their feedback about us. We need to listen … we need to hear … we need to act on what we hear.

Feedback truly **IS** the breakfast of champions. **Be a champion** …

Be an effective and respected
LEADER!

Every person I work with
knows something better
than me.
My job is to listen long
enough to find it ...
and USE it.

~Jack Nichols

ABOUT WALKTHETALK.COM

For over 30 years, WalkTheTalk.com has been dedicated to one simple goal…one single mission: *To provide you and your organization with high-impact resources for your personal and professional success.*

Walk The Talk resources are designed to:

- Develop your skills and confidence
- Inspire your team
- Create customer enthusiasm
- Build leadership skills
- Stretch your mind
- Handle tough "people problems"
- Develop a culture of respect and responsibility
- And, most importantly, help you achieve your personal and professional goals.

Contact the Walk The Talk team at
1.888.822.9255
or visit us at *www.walkthetalk.com*

Resources for Personal and Professional Success

HEY LEADER,
WAKE UP AND HEAR THE FEEDBACK

Softcover Book – $14.95
Also consider
THE LEADERSHIP DEVELOPMENT TOOL KIT

Only $49.95!

A powerful Leadership Development Resource for leaders at ALL levels.

Includes:
- *Hey Leader...Wake Up and Hear The Feedback*
- *Leadership Lessons* book – motivational quotes and inspiring leadership messages
- "Each of Us Is a Leader" DVD with an inspiring 3-minute movie on Leadership responsibilities, plus other resources
- *Lead Right* – Best-selling "straight talk guide" of practical leadership tips and techniques

The Leadership Development Tool Kit will help you and your colleagues become even more effective and respected leaders...a benefit to all leaders, their direct reports and the organizations they serve.

Visit

WALKTHETALK.COM

Resources for Personal and Professional Success

to learn more about our:

Leadership & Personal Development Center

- Develop leadership skills
- Motivate your team
- Achieve business results

Free Newsletters

- The Leadership Solution
- The Power of Inspiration
- New Products and Special Offers

Motivational Gift Books

- Inspire your team
- Create customer enthusiasm
- Reinforce core values

The Greenhouse Bookstore

- Save time
- Save money
- Save the planet

**Contact the Walk The Talk team at 1.888.822.9255
or visit us at www.walkthetalk.com.**

WALKTHETALK.COM

Resources for Personal and Professional Success